WILD BEAUTY

Alan Catlin

FUTURECYCLE PRESS
www.futurecycle.org

Cover artwork by Gene McCormick; author photo by Valerie Catlin; cover and interior book design by Diane Kistner; Gentium Book with Cronos Pro titling

Library of Congress Control Number: 2018950311

Published by FutureCycle Press
Athens, Georgia, USA

ISBN 978-1-942371-56-4

"Why is there so much trouble in the world?"
—Jeffrey Beaumont in *Blue Velvet*

Contents

1: A SIMIC SEQUENCE

2: LIFE AND DREAMS ARE PAGES OF THE SAME BOOK

3: WILD BEAUTY

1:
A SIMIC SEQUENCE

Return to a Place Lit by a Glass of Milk

after C. Simic

in a Russian winter dream
where the sleeping are more
real than the waking, the images
easier to hold on to. Where a rude
wooden table shakes but the glass
of milk remains unaffected, when
the transports go by, the warships
and cargo planes fly low over
the Forbidden Zones, the Interzones,
where the laws of physics have
been altered to accommodate
the dreamers, awake.
Here the milk shines in all kinds of weather,
radioactive as radium, as eternity
watches, their faces as hollow as cheeks
of the dead still standing in percussive
shock long after the bombs have dropped,
long after the alien intercession.
Only a child with special gifts, the habit
of levitation and the power to move minds
and objects can touch the milk, can partake
of its gifts, can see where the path it is
illuminating leads.

The Voice at 3 A.M.

after C. Simic

is the Lunatic after he has
escaped the asylum, after
he has bent the bars of a solitary
life as an acrobat would,
scribbling in the dark the code
of warped genius gone bad
on padded walls before he
finds a place to reside where
only changeling wolves
will go. Here, among friends,
he stutters, but all who gather
to hear his words know how
easily prophecy may be confused
with truth. Paintings on cave
dwelling walls tell an epic tale,
but what does it mean?

"The sun doesn't care for ambiguities,
But I do. I open my door and let them in"

—C. Simic

"Let's party!" they say,
a gaggle of them the size
of geese, rushing in.
All of them ecstatic as clowns
released from their car, waving
tiny pennants, blowing whistles,
kazoos, party hats askew as if
my place was not the first stop
on an extended tour of our
neighborhood. Once inside,
they raid the refrigerator,
the liquor cabinet, head to
the bathroom for the drugs.
Nothing I say deters them.
It's almost as if I do not belong
here, that I am an intruder
in my own home.
"Here, hold this," one of them
says to me, handing me a large
firecracker, the quarter stick of
dynamite kind. He lights the fuse
and laughs. I wait for it to go off.

"Life is haunted by its more beautiful sister life"

—C. Simic

The life exhumed from a graveyard
gone to swamp and enshrined in
a museum of dead objects, a place
the looks more like a bowling alley of
the gods than a gallery with neon
arrow hints on how to make a spare
rather than works of contemporary art.
This could be the place Alice
discovered after falling down the rabbit
hole after she stepped through her
looking glass. Even the advice given
for making spares is wrong. Still,
the flashing arrows on the otherwise
plain walls were beautiful to behold.

"When you play chess alone it's always your move"

—C. Simic

No naked women, across
the board, playing white.

No Duchamp, playing black,
hoping to expedite the checking
of his mate.

Just the men on their horses,
the bishops with their crosiers,
pawns in the field of battle
waiting their turn to die,
and the king and queen in
their proper places waiting for
what the night brings.

"The woman had a tiny smile and an open umbrella"

—C. Simic

Like a doll on wheels,
smears of rouge on
her cheeks and wax
lips that would melt
in the sun.

Her eyes are candy-
cane colored and she
has hair like cotton fluff
spun into sugary strands
that hang down her neck,
disappearing inside a
Raggedy Ann dress.

I want to ask her
what the umbrella
is for but the local
bus arrives and takes
her away.

"Your invisible friend, what happened to her?"

—*C. Simic*

They asked in such
a casual way I couldn't
tell whether they were
truly interested or whether
it was part of the interrogation.

"I honestly don't know,"
I said. It was true but no one
believed me.

"Are you homesick for the House of Cards?"

—C. Simic

She asked, leaning on
one elbow in our bed,
facing me, lips so close
I thought we might kiss.

"No," I said. "Not since
we found this cold water
flat."

"I'm glad," she said.
And I was too, though
I wasn't sure why.

"I left parts of myself everywhere
The way absent-minded people leave
Gloves and umbrellas"

—C. Simic

The way they used to make
confetti from ticker tapes
of stock market updates
and scatter them out sky-
scraper windows on special
occasion parade days.

Or the colored-paper kind
thrown at New Year's Eve
celebrations in banquet halls,
open bars and supper club
lounges where all the middle-
aged married women, and
the single mother divorced
ones, used the occasion to
lean over the bar to kiss the
young man behind it, home
numbers and times to call
scrawled on napkins furtively
passed as they kiss, as her
unexpected tongue tickles
his teeth, their eyes saying,
"I've waited all year to do
this. Let's do it again."

"Everything you didn't understand
Made you who you are"

       —C. Simic

Like the wrong turn in the supermarket
that brought you down the aisle of
lost objects: miniature Easter Island heads,
carved images of chiefs of lost tribes
of the Amazon, all the psychedelic roots
Burroughs wrote to Ginsberg about
in Yage Letters, and all the dreams they
induced. The dreams you enter into
now, clear-eyed but confused;
there are no sale items here,
no markdowns, no way out.

"The obvious is difficult
To prove. Many prefer
The hidden"

—C. Simic

What is hidden behind
the high-backed seats in
the Death Star van after
the supermarket parking
lot collision: the glass-eyed
drunk driver, the shotgun
seat companion flying higher
than the kites that flew out
on impact, and the deployed
airbags, colorful and as
buoyant as hot air balloons,
are difficult to explain.

The obvious explanation
was this was no ordinary
vehicle but what kind it was
no one could actually say.

A small voice from the
back seat area announces
that the next act of the show
begins in fifteen minutes.
We were all eager to see it.

"And even the scarecrow I once tied to a tree
So it would have to listen to me"

—C. Simic

Deserted me. And who could
blame it, really? Lectures on
Sabermetrics are difficult to
absorb even under the best of
circumstances.
Even I wasn't sure what some
of the measurements did and,
less so, what they meant.
The irony of it all is not lost
on me: a scarecrow lifted into
the air, arms spread like Christ's
as the statue in the extended aerial
shot that opens up Fellini's
La Dolce Vita. Only now,
instead of a helicopter for conveyance,
it was a flock of crows bearing the weight.

*"Always, always…we had nothing
But words"*

       —C. Simic

It's enough to make you sick
to your stomach—all those wasted
words.
Sartre wrote an autobiographical book
that he called *The Words.*
As I recall, he left out all the good
parts, the juicy stuff: all the young
groupies who wanted more than his
mind; nights with Simone after all
the drinking, the smoking, the talking
was done.
Sartre never took a candid photo
of a naked Simone the way one of her
other lovers did.
Instead he wrote *Being and Nothingness,*
and filled up all that space with hundreds
of thousands of words.

"Says she'll take him to the Museum
Of Dead Ideas and Emotions"

—C. Simic

And it will look like one of those
holy relic places, a catacomb where
votive candles by the thousand are
lit in long rows by penitents.
Nearby, in an anteroom, piles of
crutches the-no-longer-lame left
behind. And the bones, the sacred
cloaks, the cracked vessels!
What shrine would be complete
without those and a souvenir stand:
properly blessed vials of holy water,
custom-made-by-blind-people
BVMs, St. Christopher medals
for the nostalgic for the High Roman
Masses in Latin etc. believers.
For an extra charge you can see
the real good stuff they keep hidden
like carnival sideshows behind
the black curtains. To gain admittance
you must swear on the Bible not to reveal
what you have seen there.

Wedding in Hell

after C. Simic

The illustrations: before, during,
and after are court sketch artist
drawings. No photographs
for evolving triptych are allowed.

In the first panel fantastic
beasts are being formed amid
a forbidding landscape of
truculent plants and trees.
Even the skies irruptive.

In the center panel all
the perverse joys of the body
are displayed: an orgy of
succulents, nudes descending,
a slowly roasting spitted ox,
campfires and torch-bearing,
dancing demons, the witches
and the warlocks.

Final scene is of blue-black skies
scarred by lightning and fireballs.
The ground is a feculent oozing
wound and faces of revelers are
stained the color wounded soldiers
have just before death. Birds of
prey scan the sky. No one dares
to look up lest they be seen.

Book of Gods and Devils

after C. Simic

Children of the Damned prep
school boys dressed in short pants,
white shirts, and striped regimental
ties. Death-ray eyes trained to
emulsify and to kill.

Pigtailed unformed girls like
conveyor belt kids in Pink Floyd
movie slowly impelled onward
toward precipitous drop.
Their food-stained gray pleated
skirts, their pressed white blouses,
their to-die-for stares.

Blind, Our Sisters of the Poor,
sit outside anterooms of machine
factory schoolhouse doors holding
begging bowls, chanting satanic
verses, one incantation short of
a spell.

Doctors and devils and their
flat head mortarboards, their
Aramaic lesson plans, their sixty
names for God, all spelled backwards.

The World Doesn't End

after C. Simic

But prevails in free hand drawn,
flat earth, invisible city,
imaginary world maps.

Look closely at the places
people don't go: the ice-tipped
equators, sun-baked polar
caps, the dry bone ocean floors.

No one invades anyone else.
What would be the point?

The Hotel Insomnia

after C. Simic

Where all the dreamers go
when they are tired of dreaming.
All the rooms are like interiors
by Francesca Woodman:
rippled ceilings stained by leakage
and rot, sprung sash cords and
cracked panes, peeling wallpaper
no longer covering holes in wall
board, lath. Filmy wraiths,
slow exposure forms: blurred
females, naked, mottle skinned,
torsos with misshapen heads
and hair.
No faces.

2:
LIFE AND DREAMS
ARE PAGES OF THE SAME BOOK

Life and Dreams Are Pages of the Same Book

after A. Schopenhauer

The sculpted bust of the insane
man contemplating the death of
butterflies in transition is painted
in dissolving colors, warped angels,
a ruination of perspective as
destructive as macular degeneration
that clouds this likeness, this Superman's
X-ray vision, all-seeing twin death rays
no mask can contain. Inside a museum
of dead objects, the Last Supper,
an oblong table set for nine diners,
a still death, all the fruits and vegetables,
fowl and game, rotten, wilted, maggoty;
an overwhelming scent of decay
no decanted aromatic, no bottled wine
in full breath, can disguise the collapsing
bridge between the seated and the bony
structures beneath.

S. Dali's Dream of Venus

Coney Island night memories
that haven't happened yet,
a Main Street sideshow attraction
for a psychic's World's Fair
recreating a year like 1939 in
a disordered mind, uncensored
exhibits A through Z: of harems
dreaming, half-fish, half-sea
creatures on shell beds and real
ones wrapped in red satin. Venus
rising from both, stepping aside
to view the bloody Future, inside
a Cocteau mirror, where all things
dematerialize, or never were at all,
a new dimension for yellow cabs
to be hailed in, cabs with drivers
more dead than alive, listening to
broadcasts from Alpha Centauri,
their passengers heavily veiled;
behind sliding glass panels anything
is possible, even the directions to a
Grand Central Station in Hell.
You know the one with marble arches
and black arrows pointing all
the way down inside the painted deserts
of Death Valley days, arid landscapes
the unclothed dead are walking on,
bare feet not touching the sand,
hovering as if hung inside a darkening
Tunnel of Love lubricated by tears.

The Head of Mata Hari

After the firing squad execution,
the unclaimed bullet-ridden body
donated for scientific study
so bloated and brutalized by forced
inaction, incarceration without exercise,
she no longer resembled the exotic
dancer she once was, mistress of many,
of the rich and connected, masters of war,
all her slaves in the boudoir revealing
worthless secrets enemy decoders had
readily intercepted thereby removing
all her deceptive veils so that in death
she became no more than a severed head
on a silver tray, presented and preserved
in the Paris Museum of Science only
to be lost, misplaced, or stolen at some
unknown date and time, a macabre art
object in a jar of formaldehyde white as
Winged Victory's displaced head,
lids folded back to reveal eyes like
tarnished buckshot embedded in
unforgiving skin.

Spanish Exhumation

They are excavating
the unmarked graves
of a Spanish Inquisition:

mass burials by Fascists,
friends and neighbors,
fathers and sons,

men and boys
indiscriminately shot,
as immaterial now as

layers of dirt
between relics and
bones, all the same

as what is uncovered:
mostly empty wallets
identity papers

pocket watches
without hands;
life and time erased

Madame Blavatsky's Baboon

Mr. Fiske, a model of a well-respected,
upstanding citizen of the world dressed
in formal wear: black morning coat,
silk tie, and starched collar, a volume of
Darwin's *Origin of Species* held tightly
at his side, spectacles in a case for further
reading and closer study of the learned texts,
his brow creased, fire light reflected in
his cold, glass eyes, last thoughts contained
therein: the jungle's dissipating heat, the cold,
severely decorated rooms no creature should
be made to endure.

For the Angel Who Announces the End of Time

in the manner of S. Dali

This could be the world after
End Time: the sea dissolved in
sunlight, hard-baked into deserts,
exposed shells thick as colored glass
nothing is reflected in, the steel-
plated arch to nowhere sightless
birds perched upon, flexing their
bloated wings as if they were
bladders of sulfured tea.
Once punctured, a killing rain
is released, slowly descending
like some primordial ooze,
challenging the laws of gravity,
onto the unprotected heads of those
lost and wandering below,
sunstruck and amazed at the chemical hues,
sunsets that expand the view beyond
the limits of conventional sight.

Self-Portrait with Dead Flies

after a sketch by Gunter Grass

The ones that he killed when
the air they occupied was
withdrawn by an in-taken breath,
suffocation immediate, their bodies
dry husks on the table top,
winged mounds lying between
salt shakers, pepper mills, china
plates chipped along the edges
set for a beggar's banquet in
an enigmatic dream, the face of
the sleeper watching with eyes
barely open, so sorrowful, so hastily
drawn, only the lines etched into
his skin are visible.

We Are Planting the Baby Heads by Moonlight

in the rock-infested fields. Not real
baby heads, but plastic ones, found in
junkyards, burned-out buildings,
foreclosed homes. Some damaged more
than others, their pried-open eyes staring
at nothing now and the plastic sheets real
babies were changed on transmuted into
flesh for all the unseen creatures stumbling
about among the refuse, crawling on all
fours, crying out the way toddlers do to be
saved from everything let loose in the night.

We are planting the baby heads. Hoping
that with nurturing and with care, they will
grow into something fine that will be cherished
in a way that only children can be. The ones that
don't, we will leave behind to become snowmen
and women, effigies that become scarecrows
in another life, in a field like this one, where
the moon is the sun and night is day, where
all the old appliances go to die, you can hear
their coils heating, the incessant hum of the
refrigerators, the singing of the stoves.

Nightmare with Seagulls In It

They gather on pale moon-
lit nights, thousands of
them rooted in place
on the sand between the
rocks and the washed-up
weeds, the sound of their
cumulative breathing louder
than the waves as they rise
as one like skin tearing
away from a great, still
beast, their terrible wings
beating back the night sky,
blocking out the light.

Double Self-Portraits

Almost mirror images of two
young women sitting at a café
table, wineglasses half-empty,
half-full, or at the beach, in two-
piece bathing suits, one blue,
the other pink, or embracing at
the Central Park Zoo, hello,
goodbye; shadows in dark and
light like two faces becoming
one as in *Persona,* together and
apart, two aspects of the same
person, totally different, or
the dominating one becoming
the dominated as in *Passion
of Anna,* two halves of the same
whole, separate but together,
or two faces turned to a gallery wall,
impossible to tell one from the other;
two empty frames nearby where
their pictures should be.

Man Ray's Object of Destruction

A severed eye clipped to the skin
of a metronome sees everything that
has been lost: a chiaroscuro sky flushed
with blood wiped clean into a smear
of clouds by rain, a self portrait
carved from mirror glass, colored by dyes
trace elements are formed in, still lives,
waxed fruits poisoned by honeyed lacquers,
inert gases, heavy waters too polluted
to breed in, all this and more, the length
and breadth of dreaming. Cataloging the death
of love is an endless act of exposure,
negatives turned inside out like bones,
ligatures attached to layers of skin,
white calcifying humps seen bleached
and hollow as underground caves desert birds
retreat to, seeking refuge from the eyes of man.

Pastoral with Nuclear Sunset

Prevailing winds create waves
in the uncut fields, white
tips of grass gone to seed
near dusk; the multi-textured
sky, pied beauty, a dappled thing,
burnt orange on blue turning red
where the night should be.

Burning Patience

The sky at night is an opaque mirror
for watching where the wolves go,
those places just beyond the painted
murals where the horizon should be
shaded by a patchwork quilting of
abstractions, streaked with lurid colors
beneath an archway of double rainbows.
In the hour just before should-be dawn,
formative clouds are halos rising from
a hidden heat source, self-contained
beneath layers of volcanic rock and
cratered earth, shadowy as molten figures
bathed in plasma, a blanketing corset
of cumulative effects, mysterious as
sleep, or the days, that refuses to come.

Southwestern Landscape with Tears

The edge of the painted desert
ends in a plain of tears shaped
as if blown as glass in a variety
of sizes, imperfect in places,
pocked or unevenly formed,
burnished where the wind-blown
sand rubbed against the outer
surfaces; a glint of sun fractures
light into colored pieces where new
tears gather one day to replace
the older tears scratched as they
are by dust devils, sirocco, *agua*
caliente, the devil's whiskey hardened
by his breath into bastard tears,
blood spotting his sinister beard along
with the ancient ones born of embryos
that bear his infernal mark; the new ones
regenerating, a parthenogenesis,
free of the telltale signs, imprints, scars,
their saline solutions becoming glycerin,
glycerin becoming formed plastics
that will not hold the light.

La Jornada del Muerto

Bent from a lifetime of debilitating
travail, hard task making for low
wages and bad food, migrant worker
clothes marked by in-the-field labors,
fruit juice stains, brambles and thorns,
torn through to calloused-from-labors skin,
wiry arms and legs all stiff muscle
and once-broken bones, straw wide-brimmed
hat unwoven in places as if bitten or caught
en route from wherever to here amid
the split dried earth and black rock halfway
between one unforgiving place and this,
the next one.

Impossible Landscape with Common Crows

An arrangement of fruit has no
center of gravity, no resting place
to root them in the artist's eyes,
falling as they are as if hurled
from great heights, these damaged
pears, bruised apples, misshapen
bananas, black cherries cored to
the pits, seedless grapes partially
skinned, discolored fruit exposed,
all plummeting through a nebulous
emulsion, a dull, almost colorless,
almost lifeless medium, an indefinite
place for a sudden abundance of
common crows invading, their black
beaks open as if to snare plunging
fruit or to speak among themselves
of the unspeakable; this uncertainty
of place, neither up nor down, all
their hapless fluttering will neither
alter nor amend their condition.

Mud-colored Faces with False Penitents

Their upper bodies are draped
with black cloaking, partially
concealing buckskin leggings as
they gyrate in a rough circle,
arms extended above their heads,
faces smeared with brown makeup,
war paints emulating ancestral rites,
summoning dormant clouds from
a pastel sky while others kneel,
heads bent toward the rutted dirt
and dust, rough sack clothing torn
and spattered with refuse, paints
and sacrificial blood, their pale hands
torn and bruised from groveling
without surcease, unwashed strands
of dark-colored hair hanging about
their white grease-painted faces,
the taste of ash that never escapes
their lips.

Portrait of an Unreliable Witness
Surrounded by Angels

He stands, erect, bound by a loose,
encircling gold chain, painted in
the manner of a youthful, Pre-Raphaelite
poseur, wistful-looking, yearning,
unsullied face clear of any blemish,
idyllic expression suggesting false
reverence, his upturning eyes cast
heavenward but scheming, an indulgence
 of his less than pure senses, tempted by
the flesh of unholy angels, the near naked
ones clothed in diaphanous white robes,
holding platters of steaming meats,
goblets of wine, scented amulets, and
aphrodisiac potions in this strange,
unidentifiable outdoor place before
the rapture, the silent music of stars.

Interior with Young Man
Standing on a Window Ledge

Here, at the convergence of walls,
two windows, the closed one, double-
hung casements, bottom panel opaque,
upper filled by pale blue sky, a fringe
of cumulus, the open one, on our right,
is where the young man has crawled out
onto the building ledge where he stands,
looking up at something unseen without
clear intent, neither anxious nor
unnatural, strangely relaxed seeming,
his empty briefcase hanging loosely
from the wrist of his visible right hand,
desk in the interior foreground, clear,
polished not even a blotter just a computer
monitor, screen saver by Magritte: a brown-
suited man wearing a black derby hat,
staring at a falsely blue sky within,
a telephone desk ensemble unplugged
suggesting: NO INCOMING CALLS TODAY.

Man Bent Over Wristwatch
of Dead Boss

kneeling on concrete sidewalk,
Rolex removed from limp wrist
stained by blood spatters, smears
on grey summer suit coat sleeve,
white, embroidered with initials
shirt clearly visible though the man's
head is not, is hidden by special pages
of a *Wall Street Journal,* his employee
considering the removed object as a
talisman, a trinket, a spoil of some
undeclared war fought just this side
of the grave.

Still Life with Severed Hand
and Forged Painting

The hand, a right one, lies palm
side up, useless fingers bent in
a near clutching cup as if holding
an invisible globe, a ball of some
sort, a tarnished gold ring facing
outward on the third finger for signets,
franking no more, lifelines crosshatched
and scarred, wrist seared black
at the point of severance, a defaced
portrait of a young noble lady staring
downward, hooded eyes nearly closed,
thin lips unnaturally white within this dark
interior marred by scored red linings,
black singeing ash.

Still Life with Ghost of Angry Ancestor

One place is set at the head
of the antique formal dining table:
a white lace cloth embroidered with
coats-of-arms, heraldic imagery, a fading
powder-blue coverall, bone china
and golden cutlery slightly out of place
as if used and set aside, a hint and
a smear, a stain on the plate, a suggestion
of a ring about the cup, decanted wine,
full-bodied and breathing, the snuffed
candles, blackened wicks bent,
forced down near the hardened, melted wax,
a shimmering, indistinct figure hovering
just above the thickly padded, high-backed
chair at the table head, desiccated fruit
in a crystal bowl on a sideboard nearby:
Anjou pears, blood oranges and apples,
withered grapes, hard-as-rock dates
and figs, blackened berries; what the old
one once touched, now lies dead.

Market in Dutch Town with Phony Eskimo

after Van Eyck

Wily black clad merchants at
outdoor market hold polished
trinkets in their gnarled hands,
aging faces furrowed by years
of bartering for the best prices,
high cheek bones of the leaner
one suggests shrewdness and a
flatterer's hard bargaining pose,
soft spoken empty phrases formulating
behind feral eyes, pinched lips
caressing a lupine smile while
the larger, stout burgher indicates
worthless baubles inset with semi-
precious stones to an unseen prospective,
his ruddy cheeks belie false health
and good humors, nearby a stuffed
relic of foreign travels sits propped
against the wooden stalls draped
with worn clothing, something clearly
humanoid but not the as-advertised
aborigine from Northern climes brought
back for natural science, study and
edification, but a cheap imitation made
from rags and stuffing carefully shaped
and molded as a waxen likeness of man,
suitable for entertainment purposes only.

Athanasius Kircher Seated on a Crocodile Composing His Encyclopedic Works

Kircher, the man, the high priest, is a living
specimen in a divine cabinet of curiosities.
Runic scripts evolve from his fingertips,
his quill pens; all the mysteries of ancient
tongues are supposed to be revealed with.
This man, part-magus, part-monk, writes on,
his creations legion: solar clocks
from magic seeds, rune stones and
monkey dust curatives and salves for
all that ails, inventions and novelties
such as vomiting statues and pianoforte-like
instruments using living cats to produce
torturous sounds supposed to be like music,
spy portals in revolving carved heads,
sound amplifiers in other busts, altered to
allow listeners to overhear conversations
in remote locations, owner of Egyptian relics
actually made in Rome, misdated by
a millennium, practical theories of convection
formulated firsthand viewing volcanoes
from within, a research only a holy fool
could survive, whole volumes of inscribed
work, catalogs of presumed fact, completely
borrowed, wholesale copied from other scholar's
work, most, if not all of his own, disproved
even as he wrote on. This man in his element,
endlessly amazed as he was amazing, surrounded
by angels, sun gods and goddesses, half-dragons
and half-snakes, a man so self-possessed
only death could save him from himself.

Schopenhauer's Cosmic Dreamer
Dreaming the Dream of the Universe

Here the sculpted man twisted into
fetal knots, roughage removed
from imperfect stone, an occluded
vein hammered into submission,
chiseled until the hardest places
are like sleep running as ice melt
will when exposed to direct light or
a ripple of reflected moonlight
hardened into fingers cradling still
forming embryos of dream becoming
that penultimate place where white noise is
filtered through raw cavities of rain
gradually assuming shapes that blacken
an endless waste of stillborn night;
all those sickening hours before dawn
neighborhood outlaws are compelled to
assemble shooting stars for the next wave
of temperature inversions, of self-
containment within hard glass globes
fraught by artificial weathering—
a man is a mean object here, created
only to be scorned, known only by
the acid rain that settles in the hollow
crevices, the empty sockets of his eyes.

3:
WILD BEAUTY

Wild Beauty in the Mind of the Living

"Language is how ghosts enter the world"
—Anne Michaels

How could the artist stare at
himself in the mirror? The one
missing ear covered by bandages
soiled by oil paints, tinctured
alcohol, visions distilled from absinthe
flavored sugar cubes extracted from
glass fragments, burnt umbers for blood
and pallid pastes for bone making
potato eaters out of magistrates,
judges defenseless before the law,
everyone guilty as charged, equally
damaged by a slashing strike,
vital fire withdrawn from each furtive,
expressive eye, a canvas colored
gastric green amid the yellowing fever,
a murder of crows foretold, the ones
that carry plague rat ticks instead
of well-ripened cherries from a midnight
garden of earthly delights.

Some Comfort Gained from the Acceptance of the Inherent Lies of Everything

*"There are doors that slam louder than
mortar rounds that have landed on a face"*
—Bill Shields

She comes back for me from the place
where she died in a dream of 1985,
eyes lit by Roman candles time-releasing
synthetic balls of fire inside eyes
marbleized harder than tempered
glass, body wasted by fatal cancers,
knotted inside, tighter than bolls of Black
Forest trees she whispered of, creating
new songs without words to be played on
string instruments forever out of tune,
a new *Mephisto Waltz* the goal of all
her frantic composing on the other side,
the rotten apples for her son held out
on hands made brittle by the cold,
the dark placing of herself within
the Arctic plane of memory, the awful fact
of the truth as she wrote it, "Old Age is
a fraud and Death is a lie!" something not
easily dispelled in this life or the other,
though the nightmare only truly began where
it ended in life, in fire, as if it were my
truest wish, behind a crematory door.

The Physical Impossibility of Death
Within the Mind of Someone Living

"What did we care—we were young and had
no interest in the personal problems of corpses"
—Jack Evans

The old folks remember how it was
before the chainsaw artists cut
the dead calves in half, exposing
all the organs for scientific display
or conversationally piecing together
anatomic disparities with diseased
medicines for melancholy, "Here is
where necrosis begins," they say,
pointing at the suspected, the infected
part, "and this is how it ends"—as a deformity,
a grotesque, suspended in a solution,
floating weightless, something from another
existence, more alien than the failure
of space and time combined, one blind,
embalmed eye focused on the last true
moment; these men dressed all in white,
pull-starting chainsaws, just beyond
the charnel house doors.

"Hieronymus Bosch put his finger on the wound"

—Terry Tempest Williams

drew the lines for anatomists to follow,
exposing hidden sutures, internal formication
for those possessed by seizures, see them mesmerizing
the wings from dead angels, draining life fluids
from archaic monsters summoned into being
by evil spirits released from another world;
once their tongues have been removed, their eyes
poked through with sticks, who will remain
to articulate their spent visions?
who will paint the future?

A Shark in the Mind of Someone Contemplating Wilderness

"Blood, that euphemism for what moves us"
—Anne Michaels

What moves between the unfleshing
of the bones, those internal organs
left to float in briny emulsion, diseased
as medicinal waste discarded before
the self-immolation of flamed bodies,
singed by lab coat porters swathed in
prophylactic plastic, armored against
latent plagues of viral dreams;
what moves within the blackened pitch
of divers eddying amid insurgent tidal
breaks, an energy of fits contained within
Precambrian eyes too dull with impulse,
instinctual needs, to be considered savage
or willful, consuming skinned prey,
the suspended, inanimate, a bloat of infective
tissue spired on a cantilever of internal light;
what moves the compressed jaws of great
whites, the hammerheads, masticating dead
museums of the heart, deadening the nerves,
enrapturing the deep, hastening the funneling
drain into the unfathomable brightness
of light? A shark moves at the end
of the mind, patrolling postdiluvian lands,
sandcastles built for the restive dead,
condemned to a post-life of eternal suicide,
a wilderness of dreams.

The Actual Existence of Really Important
Meaning of What Happens to Man over Time

The ancestors are singing the old
songs of significance locked in the hard-
packed earth, the false light of caves
glowing in the neon bones of their faces
pressed within the cordite-rich chambers
charged and ready to be fired, coffined
urns on the edges of columbarium,
iconography impressed within, the runes
of sages languaging the past with key
phrasings beyond understanding, a locus
of death and dying, fringed shawls
of mourning draped about the hollowed
skulls devising a mute for solo voices
forced upon the wind, the bleak painted
deserts, where no man comes.

The Nature of Things

after Cristina Vergano

as contained in philosopher's stones
is what the half-ape, half-serpent,
bipedal man is trying to formulate
a language for. All the guides left
by Alchemists past, present, and future
tell the same story in different tongues:
scrolled on paper as texts as in an
Egyptian Book of the Dead or written
on wind currents that disturb what was
once imperturbable, lost wonders of
an ancient world: Hanging Gardens
of Babylon, Colossus of Rhodes,
the Lighthouse of Alexandria,
Statue of Zeus, Oracle of Delphi,
all the conventional knowledge of
the world contained in one central
repository attended by butterflies,
impossible reptilian birds, white skulls
that speak of long-forgotten worlds,
what is and what is not contained by fire:
The Great Pyramids of Giza, riddles
of the silent Sphinx, black smoke at
Mediterranean's edge, the cosmic eggs
that refuse to float.

Ptolemy, Darwin, and Aristotle

Three panels of a Bosch-like
triptych show a contiguous landscape,
not a Garden of Earthly Delights
but something less exacting
such as an Alchemist's dream of
natural secrets, partially revealed
and inexactly understood.
The center frame dominated by
a speculative science; evolution as
an active art, purposeful and vibrant
as the new volcano spewing smoke
prior to a massive eruption, one that
might set back the course of near
human events a millennia or more.
Oblivious to radical changes at this
last minute, the armadillo-like creature
appears not only sentient but wise
beyond his partial development into
a fully endowed, human life form.
His prehensile hands are unnaturally
large especially in relation to vestigial
arms that seem grafted to the body
as an obscene cosmic joke not unlike
the one being perpetrated by Creator
through systematic disinformation
disseminated as Fact. The known world,
at this time, is represented by a fixed
earth surrounded by spherical rings
in accordance with plans sketched in
invisible inks by Aristotle's Other:
a monkey pressing closely against
the rune tablet of mysterious knowledge,
a writing nemesis looking back

from his panel as if guilty of some
unimaginable logistical mistake,
one the meager cumulative knowledge
of man cannot ameliorate or correct,
as the third panel suggests, in the form
of a hourglass almost out of Time,
shakily balanced on a pile of weighty
tomes, books of revelation and of
knowledge, balanced in turn on rounded
back of an ancient giant tortoise
crawling deliberately toward this
pseudo-Darwin to deliver a partial
gift of discovery, knowing full well
that it is too late in terms of evolution,
is the equivalent of: not evolved at all.

Unnaming the Animals

All the common ones have been
released: Tricorns and Saber Tooths,
Wooly Mammoth, Yakosaurs and
Alligoats, Pan American jungle scenes
like an Exhibit A of an evolutionary
crime scene: white spiders hollowing
petrified wood, commandeering flexible
bones of the deceased for plant life,
burning crystals in lieu of full moon light,
recruiting arachosaurs, larger than most
carnivores, as guards against intruding elements:
the improbable meat-eating tree sloths,
vegetable eaters of the dead, planet
primeval a Garden of Earthly Delights,
a brave new bathospheric place for
the unformed and the formless assuming
shifting shapes; all these banished creatures
in full retreat, represented just beyond Eden,
leaderless, climbing still hot, new-formed,
volcanic rock, a wizened sage drawing
the map of their retreat along with a treasury
one outlining outer boundaries of this crucible
of modern life in full flux, X marking spots
on parchment where nothing connects.

The Telephone

"This would be hell, I thought"
—Kevin Brockmeier

rings, ringing in the living room,
the study, the mudroom, ringing
in the basement, in the bedroom
near where you are lying, immobile,
paralyzed somewhere between waking
and sleep, ringing on landlines,
cordless phones, cells, insistent,
urgent, everywhere at once, more
phones ringing than you own, could
ever own, would ever own, ringing
here and everywhere else you have
ever lived, would ever live, even
the phone in your missing child's
room, the one you feel you must
pick up, hoping to hear her voice;
holding a Playskool toy against
yourself as if it were her body,
the one you will never see again,
reaching for you, speaking to you
across an unbreachable gulf.

Lisette Model's Feet

In the darkroom, taking shape
from negative light, thousands
of pairs of bare feet, some
reclining, bottom sides out,
unclad for beachfronts, wrinkles
describing lifelines, spent pleasures,
glorious defects, others tagged at
the right big toe, named or
unknown, still others captured
from above, taken waist-high,
bones revealed close to the flesh,
veined and gnarled by misuse,
carbuncular, scarred, tattooed
yin and yang on opposite sides,
some cut by surgeries, others
not at all, mates to the millions
of unmatched shoes left by
soon-to-be-dead men and women
walking along the main highway
just before the fall of Saigon.

"Outside the rain has brought up worms"

after a line by Ruth Stone

rising as black fingers
escaping the night soiled

earth, hydrotropic no more,
they squirm as if shocked

awake in their collapsing
tunnels by an unseen force,

galvanic energies, stimulating
new nerve endings, attachments

to a shed of skin, elapsed in
their collective terrors under

ground; the remaining stumps
of deserted hands are relinquished in

their graves, unencumbered by
needs that may easily be grasped,

their futures becoming hard,
immovable as rock.

"I am no longer human in the rain"

after a line by Gabriella Gutierrez y Muhs

but something discarded,
part animal, part beast,

a freak empowered with
the wisdom of fears,

shunned,
battered,

worn,
and made effigial

after all the burning rites
are completed,

the bad medicine,
gris-gris gone awry,

savage mojo misapplied,
a fetish for the voodoo woman

to clamp to her chest
with stick pins and razor blades,

casting unthinkable spells,
plagues of unreason.

Reading futures in
the entrails of

the sacrificed requires
six senses and a third

eye for seeing
the butcher's reward,

beheaded chicken flocks,
blood spurting dreams,

an alien rain turning
cloud births into dust.

Dream Catchers

hung as wind-
chimes on
back lit porches

swayed by
imperceptible
tidal shifts,

lunar moods
spraying
moon dust,

interior lights
turning
metallic music

makers into
fingers,
toxic creepers,

tentative vines,
sprouted tentacles
whose touch

withers spines,
drains
the life out

of stillborn
sleepless
nights

"The gaze of ice, as if snowmen made Neanderthal"

after a line by Clayton Eshleman

in the morning
they were gone

the bones of their
memories sunk
into tidal pools,

dead seas

flying fish
drank from
and became buoyant,

their breath
the fog
that brought

polar winds,
dry ice;

cave painters
tell a different
story

In the Garden of Damaged Teeth

attendant farmers are dentists
in worn overalls, stained by
tartar dark as the loam used
to fertilize fields of black ice
Northern Lights illuminate
long after the midnight sun has
settled on the horizon as a
beacon for dead sailors to
navigate now that damaged teeth
have risen as ice floe, glacial crops
laid out in orderly rows; molars,
hollow crypts, safe havens
for flocks of white crows,
molting shadows that cast aside
pale feathers leached of enamel,
mineral content, pointed incisors
plinths, eye teeth stoma for
memorial arches, statues rendered
in the likeness of a no longer
human race, their consecrated
resting places, burial mounds
linked by caves excavated just below
gum lines, the ruined walls, where
bloodstains of martyred virgins
take root and flourish as commemorative
wreathes, floribunda, purple flowers
that have no name.

Van Gogh's Dream of Easter Islands

At ocean's edge,
receding cliffs,

beach sand, clay darkened

and rust stained.
On nearly submerged rocks,

the extended black wings
of shore birds envelop

the sun, are a canvas
of wind-ruffled feathers

painted stars are created on;
each one represents

a dead spirit lost in
a vain search for sky.

Self-Portrait as the Devil's Disciple

Out of time and place,
in his bedroom, a still

life of empty bottles,
spilled wine and turpentine,

swabs of paint left
on wood floors like

trails of blood leading
to a landscape with rain,

leading to a rutted highway
of one way signs that lead

to a forest scene with
two figures: an undertaker

and his ghost.

Acknowledgments

Abbey: "'Always, always...we had nothing...'"

Argestes: "Burning Patience"

Art Mag: "S. Dali's Dream of Venus"

Bitter Oleander: "Southwestern Landscape with Tears," "Schopenhauer's Cosmic Dreamer Dreaming the Dream..."

Blue Fifth Review: "'Outside the rain has brought up worms'"

Creativity Webzine: "'Hieronymus Bosch put his finger on the wound,'" "Hotel Insomnia"

Edgz: "Dream Catchers"

5 AM: "Self-Portrait with Dead Flies"

Ginosko Literary Journal: "Return to a Place Lit by a Glass of Milk," "'The sun doesn't always care for ambiguities...,'" "'Life is haunted by its more beautiful sister life...,'" "'I left parts of myself everywhere...,'" "'Everything you didn't understand...'"

Glass Tesseract: "Still Life with Severed Hand," "Still Life with Ghost of Angry Ancestor"

Homestead Review: "Wild Beauty in the Mind of the Living"

Hunger Magazine: "Market with Dutch Town and Phony Eskimos," "Small Comfort Gained from the Acceptance of the Inherent Lies in Everything," "The Physical Impossibility of Death within the Mind of Someone Living," "Ptolemy, Darwin and Aristotle," "Unnaming the Animals"

Kind of a Hurricane Press: "Dreams of Venus," "For the Angel Who Announces the End of Time"

Milk Magazine: "Impossible Landscape with Common Crows"

Minotaur: "The Head of Mata Hari"

New Verse News: "Pastoral with Nuclear Sunset"

Parting Gifts: "Nightmare with seagulls in it," "Interior with Young Man on a Ledge," "Man Bent Over Watch with Dead Boss," "Lisette Model's Feet"

Pedestal Magazine: "Man Ray's Object of Destruction"

Presa Press: "A Shark in the Mind of Someone Living"

Rhino Literary Journal: "In the Garden of Damage Teeth"

Sheila-Na-Gig: "The Telephone"

Skidrow Penthouse: "Double Self-Portrait"

Tiger's Eye: "Mud Colored Penitents with False Prophets"

Zillah: "La Jornada del Muerto," "Portrait of Unreliable Witness Surrounded by Penitents"

ZYX: "'Life and dreams are pages of the same book...,'" "The Nature of Things," "'I am no longer human in the rain,'" "Van Gogh Dreams of Easter Islands"

About FutureCycle Press

FutureCycle Press is dedicated to publishing lasting English-language poetry books, chapbooks, and anthologies in both print-on-demand and Kindle ebook formats. Founded in 2007 by long-time independent editor/publishers and partners Diane Kistner and Robert S. King, the press incorporated as a nonprofit in 2012. A number of our editors are distinguished poets and writers in their own right, and we have been actively involved in the small press movement going back to the early seventies.

The FutureCycle Poetry Book Prize and honorarium is awarded annually for the best full-length volume of poetry we publish in a calendar year. Introduced in 2013, our Good Works projects are anthologies devoted to issues of universal significance, with all proceeds donated to a related worthy cause. Our Selected Poems series highlights contemporary poets with a substantial body of work to their credit; with this series we strive to resurrect work that has had limited distribution and is now out of print.

We are dedicated to giving all of the authors we publish the care their work deserves, making our catalog of titles the most diverse and distinguished it can be, and paying forward any earnings to fund more great books.

We've learned a few things about independent publishing over the years. We've evolved a unique, resilient publishing model that allows us to focus mainly on vetting and preserving for posterity poetry collections of exceptional quality without becoming overwhelmed with bookkeeping and mailing, fundraising activities, or taxing editorial and production "bubbles." To find out more about what we are doing, come see us at www.futurecycle.org.

The FutureCycle Poetry Book Prize

All full-length volumes of poetry published by FutureCycle Press in a given calendar year are considered for the annual FutureCycle Poetry Book Prize. This allows us to consider each submission on its own merits, outside of the context of a contest. Too, the judges see the finished book, which will have benefitted from the beautiful book design and strong editorial gloss we are famous for.

The book ranked the best in judging is announced as the prize-winner in the subsequent year. There is no fixed monetary award; instead, the winning poet receives an honorarium of 20% of the total net royalties from all poetry books and chapbooks the press sold online in the year the winning book was published. The winner is also accorded the honor of being on the panel of judges for the next year's competition; all judges receive copies of all contending books to keep for their personal library.

www.ingramcontent.com/pod-product-compliance
Lightning Source LLC
Chambersburg PA
CBHW070009100426
42741CB00012B/3167